Puzzling Optical Illusions

by
Thomas Crawford

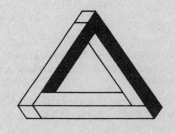

DOVER PUBLICATIONS, INC.
Mineola, New York

Copyright

Published in Canada by General Publishing Company, Ltd., 30 Lesmill Road, Don Mills, Toronto, Ontario.

Bibliographical Note

Puzzling Optical Illusions is a new work, first published by Dover Publications, Inc., in 1999.

Library of Congress Cataloging-in-Publication Data

Crawford, Tom, 1941–
    Puzzling optical illusions / Tom Crawford.
        p. cm. — (Dover game and puzzle activity books)
    ISBN 0-486-40151-0 (pbk.)
    1. Optical illusions. I. Title. II. Series.

QP495 .C73 1999
152.14'8—dc21   99-042487

Manufactured in the United States of America
Dover Publications, Inc., 31 East 2nd Street, Mineola, N.Y. 11501

Introduction

What is an optical illusion? An optical illusion is something that isn't there. Our eyes see it, but it doesn't actually exist. Everyone has heard stories about thirsty travelers in the desert who think they see an oasis up ahead with shady palm trees and cool water to drink. Unfortunately, when they get there, the oasis doesn't really exist. It is an optical illusion caused by atmospheric conditions in the desert and the traveler's brain hoping really hard to find an oasis.

How does an optical illusion happen? When you see, your eyes transmit images from the retinas in the back of your eyes to your brain. The brain then interprets what it sees. Have you ever looked at a bright light, then closed your eyes and seen an image of the light still there? That is another kind of illusion caused by the image of the light remaining on your retinas so that your brain continues to see a light. Gradually, the image disappears.

In this book you'll find many other kinds of optical illusions. The illusions are caused by different things. Some are caused by shortcomings in our vision, but most are the result of our eyes playing tricks on our brains. Based on past experience, the brain interprets the messages from our eyes in a certain way. If we then "change the rules," so to speak, the brain may have difficulty in figuring out what it's seeing. The result is an optical illusion. Although scientists have studied optical illusions for years, they are still not sure how some of them work! This book is your opportunity to discover and explore the fascinating world of puzzling optical illusions!

Answers to some of the questions asked in this book appear upside down at the bottom of the page.

The Necker Cube

This is a famous visual illusion first described by L. A. Necker in 1832. If you stare at it for a moment, you'll notice that the cube seems to tilt, first one way, then another.

Vase or Faces

Do you see an elegant white vase or two dark faces in profile?

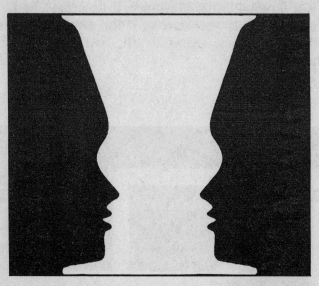

This or That

Concentrate on the black areas; what do you see? Now focus on the white areas; do you see something different?

Impossible Prongs

This is called an impossible figure. At first it seems normal, but if you look closely, you'll see it could not actually exist.

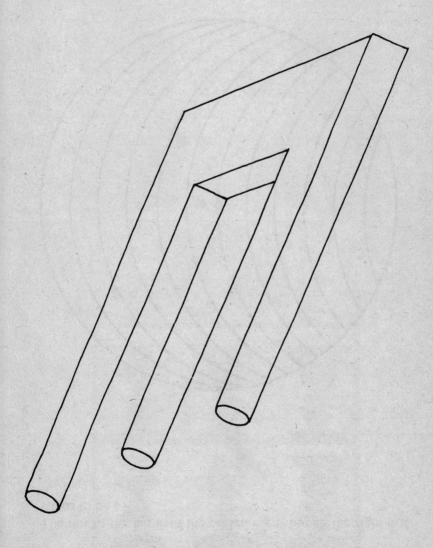

Dots Hard to Believe!

Which dot is at the center of these circles?

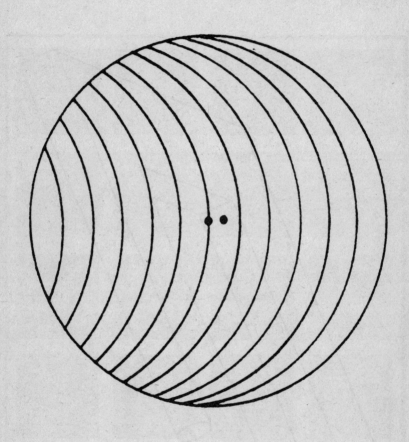

The dot to the left is in the center, even though the right dot seems to be.

Spotted Grid

Look at this grid for a moment. Do you see gray spots at the intersections of the white strips? Are they really there?

There are actually no dots there. Try to look directly at one and you'll see it disappear.

Up the Down Staircase

If you gaze at this staircase for a while, it will suddenly turn upside down. It helps to look at the near end of a step and imagine it at the far end.

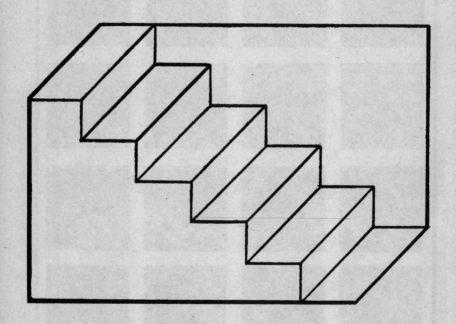

Puzzling Patterns

Does this illustration show a white pattern on a black background or a black pattern on a white background? After looking at it for a moment, you may find it hard to decide!

Confusing Circles

Is the circle in the center of the small circles bigger than the circle in the center of the large circles?

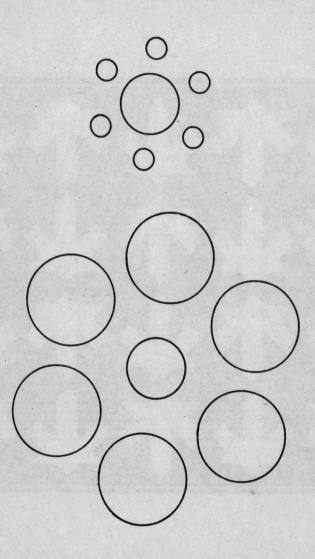

It just appears that way. Both circles are the same size.

Imperfect Circle?

What's wrong with this circle?

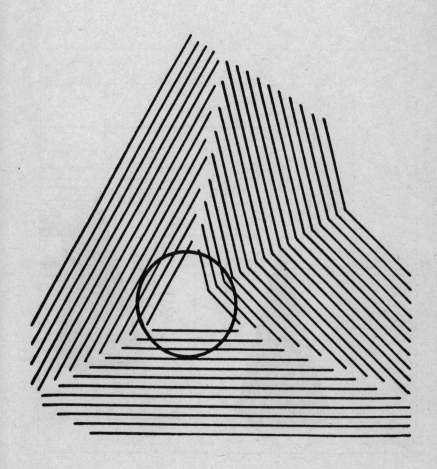

Nothing at all. It is perfectly round. The lines around it make it appear distorted.

Corridor Cones
Which cone appears larger?

Because of the perspective of the corridor, the cone farthest away appears larger, but the cones are actually the same size.

Pop Goes the Pattern

If you look at this collection of white dots, you'll suddenly see the dots form themselves into such geometric patterns as triangles, circles and trapezoids.

Carpenter's Nightmare

It's possible to draw this crate on paper but impossible to actually build one.

Silly Stilts
Are the stilts the clown is standing on wobbly or straight?

The grid behind the lines makes them appear wobbly but they are actually straight.

Over the Line

Which line is longest: the line from A to B or the line from A to C?

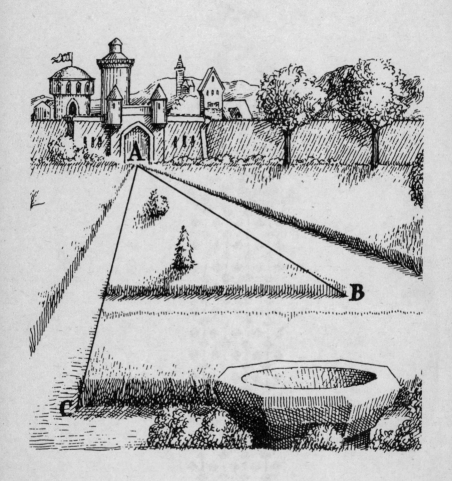

If you measure them, you'll find the lines are the same length.

Beetle Mania

At first, the beetle seems to be on the outside of the box. But if you stare at it for a moment or two, suddenly the beetle is on the *inside* of the box!

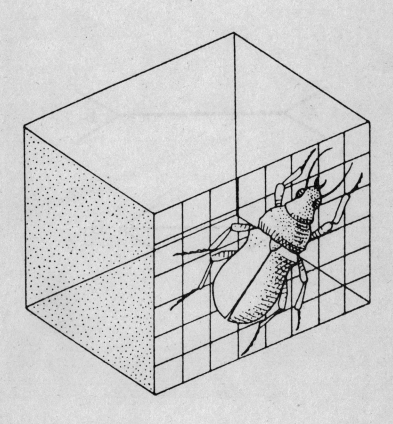

The Long and the Short of It
Which line is longer—A to B, or C to D?

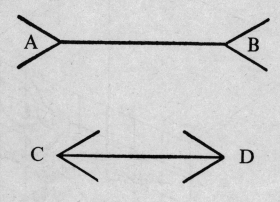

The angles at the ends make the lines appear unequal but they're actually the same length.

Surprising Shapes

Which shape is bigger, A or B?

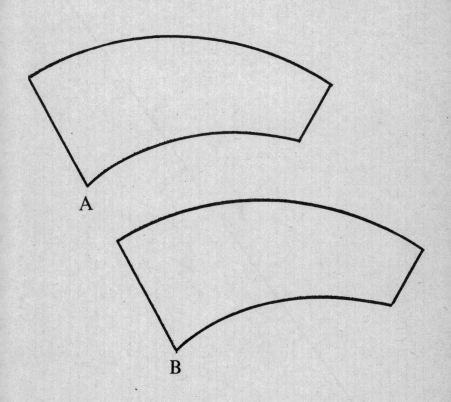

A

B

Out of Line?

Is the diagonal line in this illustration absolutely straight or does it seem to jump around a little between the vertical lines?

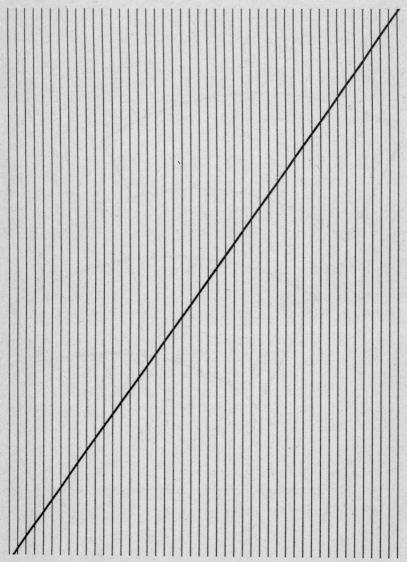

It's straight. The vertical lines make it seem slightly crooked.

Looking for an Angle

Which of these two angles is bigger, A or B?

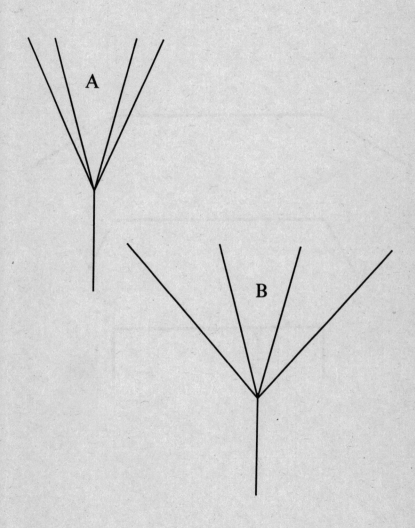

They're both the same size. The angles on either side make
them seem unequal.

19

Tricky Lines

Look at the three horizontal lines in this picture. Which is the longest?

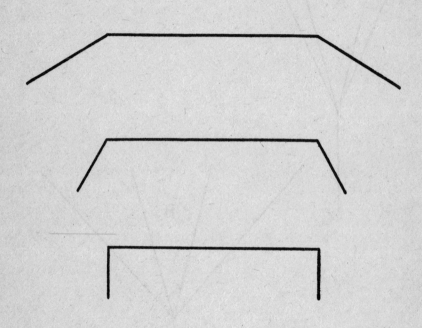

Don't let the different angles fool you. The lines are all of equal length.

Bend and Wobble

Are the vertical lines in this illustration bending and wobbling?

If you place a straightedge along the lines, you'll find they're perfectly straight. The zig-zag lines in the background make them appear to bend.

Centered Circles

Is one of the circles in the center bigger than the other?

It just seems that way because of the different sizes of the surrounding circles. Both inner circles are of equal size.

Moving Target

If you look at this illustration long enough, it will appear to revolve. Why?

The cause is eye fatigue. The eye tries to look at all the lines at once, but because the lines are so close together, the eye tires and the resulting fatigue produces the illusion of motion.

Battle of the Bulges
What makes this page look full of bulges?

By making the black squares progressively larger a bulging illusion is created on the flat surface of the page.

24

Put on Your Glasses

Look at the straight lines in these pictures of eyeglasses and a dumbbell. Which is longer?

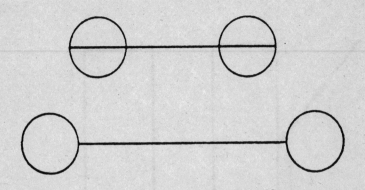

Both straight lines are the same length.

Straight Arrow

Is the dot in the center of the arrow?

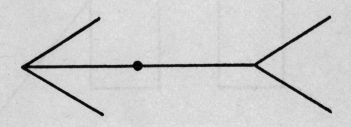

Although it looks like it is closer to the left, the dot is exactly in the center.

Shifting Diagonals

Do you see three separate lines behind the standing rectangles?

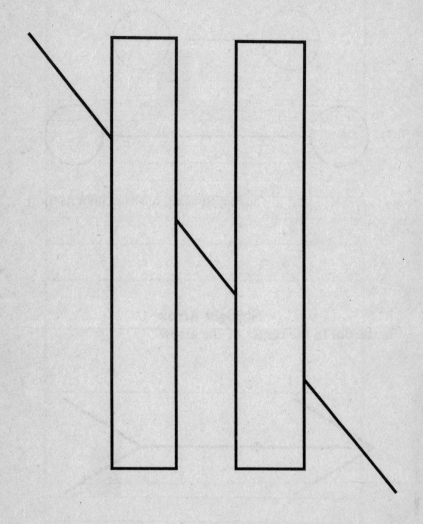

If you place a straightedge along the diagonal lines you'll see they are three parts of the same line.

Rectangle Riddle

Which of the two rectangles in this picture is the biggest?

If you guessed the top one, guess again. Both rectangles are the same size.

People Parade

Which of these three figures is the tallest?

Even though the one farthest away looks the biggest, they're all the same size. The perspective of the corridor makes them appear unequal.

Top Hat

Is this hat taller than it is wide? What do you find when you check it with a ruler?

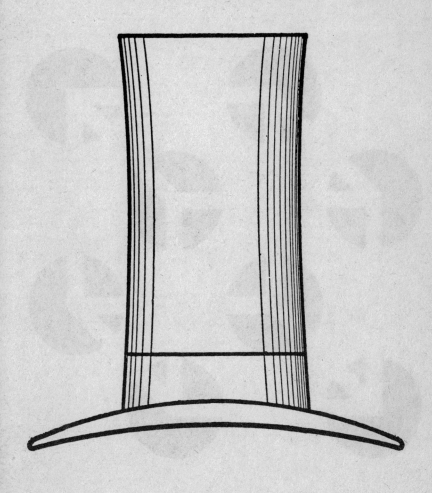

The height and width are exactly the same, even though it looks taller.

Cube-a-Dots
Is there really a cube floating over the eight dots?

There actually is no cube. The shape is only suggested by the
pattern on the black dots.

Crazy Cubes

Is the black on the top or bottom of each cube? If you stare at this picture for a few moments, you'll see the cubes do flip-flops.

Step Lively

Try and find the top and bottom steps in this picture.

Give up? You can't find them because the picture is an impossible figure.

Square Deal

Does the top square look as though its sides are bulging out? Do the sides of the bottom one seem to be sagging inward?

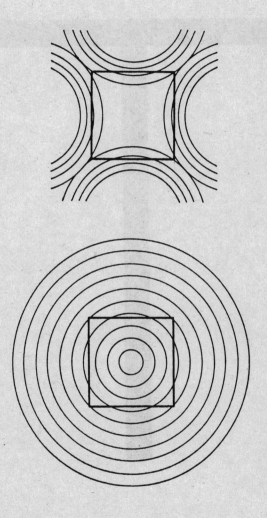

"T" Time
Is the vertical bar longer than the top bar?

The bars are both the same length. But a vertical bar always gives the illusion of being longer than a horizontal bar.

Bulges and Bends

Look carefully at the white bars in these pictures. Are they straight or do they seem to bulge and bend?

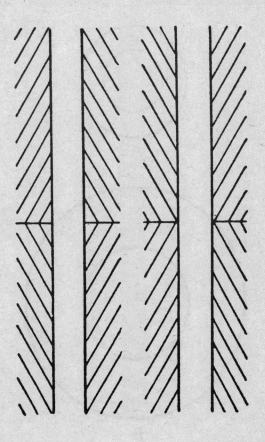

The bars are perfectly straight.

Tricky Circles

Is the inside circle of "b" larger than the outside circle of "a"?

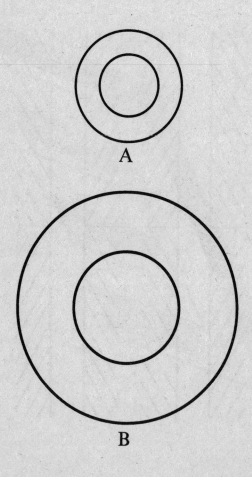

A

B

That Sinking Feeling!

Look carefully at this figure for about 30 seconds. Is it sinking down or falling toward you?

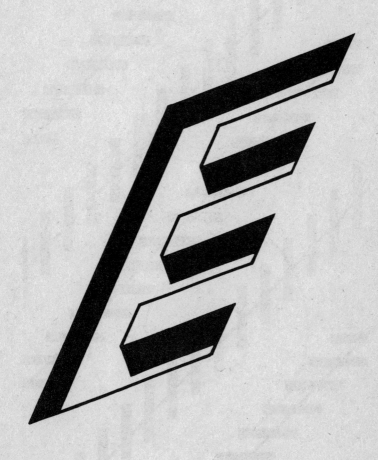

Actually, it can be seen both ways depending how you look at it.

Parallel Perspective

Are the thin lines veering all over the place, or are they perfectly parallel?

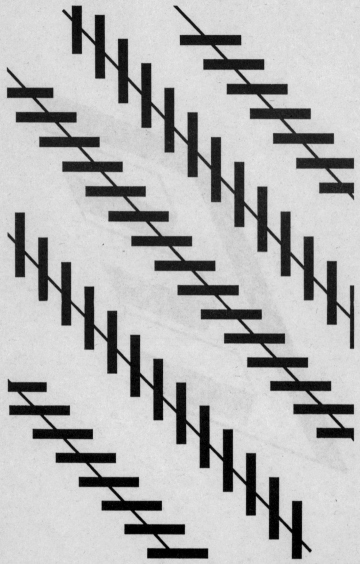

Surprise! The vertical and horizontal bars make the parallel lines appear crooked.

Puzzling Cubes

Do you scc 6 or 4 cubes?

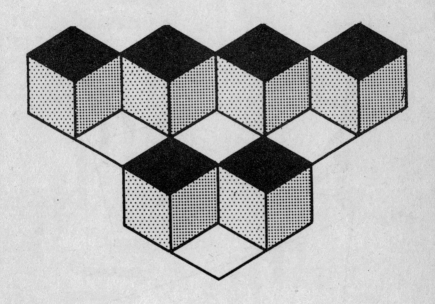

Both numbers are correct. It depends on whether you see the cubes as having white bottoms or black tops.

Cliff Hanger

One of these men must be suspended in mid air—but which one?

It could be either, depending on which area you perceive as the cliff.

Arching Circles

Are these circles really curving upward, or are they flat on the surface?

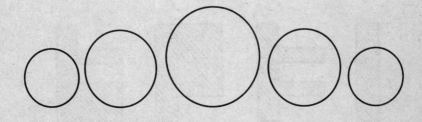

Place a straightedge along the bottom of the circles and you'll find that they're flat, despite what they look like.

Mrs. Feemster's Message

This is a work of sculpture by an artist named Elinor Louise Feemster. Do you know what she's trying to say?

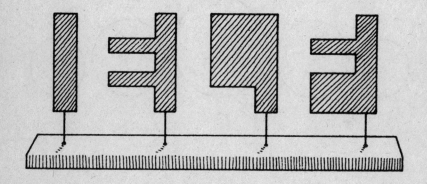

The white spaces between the four shaded pieces spell out her initials.

What's the Angle?

Is one of the circles in the angle larger than the others?

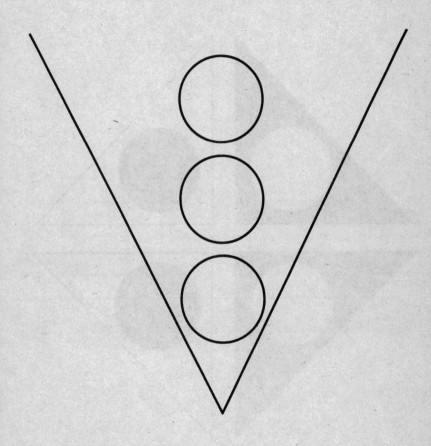

Because of its position in the angle, the bottom circle appears larger. The circles are all the same size.

Circles, Circles, Circles

Which of the four circles are the same size?

TOP

BOTTOM

In the top row, both circles are the same size, although the white one looks larger. In the bottom row, both look the same size, but the black circle is actually larger.

44

Puzzling Picture Frame

If you gaze at this picture frame for a few moments, you'll notice something strange: it seems to flip back and forth!

Mystery Figures

Are the black sides inside or out?

It could be either.

What do you see in this picture?

A white square that's not really there!

46

Tricky Spirals

One of these spirals consists of a single piece of rope with its ends joined. The other consists of two separate pieces of rope, each with joined ends. Try to find out which is which just by using your eyes. Using a pencil is cheating!

The single rope is on the left

Confusing Curves

Do you see circles or ovals in this picture?

They are all circles. The swirling checkerboard background
makes it seem as though some are ovals.

Mystery Man

Who is this very famous American? The farther away you hold the picture, the clearer it becomes.

Abraham Lincoln.

Tricky Trees

Which tree appears closer to you?

Because they are on a flat piece of paper, both trees are the same distance from you, but because dark things tend to look farther away, the lighter tree seems closer.

Square Deal

Does one of these squares seem a little bigger than the other?

Although the white square appears slightly larger, both squares are exactly the same size.

Do You Read What You See?

Read this sentence carefully. What's wrong?

A BIRD IN THE
THE HAND IS WORTHLESS.

The word "the" appears twice.

Young or Old?

What do you see in this picture?

You can see either a young woman (head turned) or an old one (looking down).

Lineup
Which of the two thin lines is the longest?

Topsy Turvy!

If you look at this picture right side up, it appears to be a woman's head. But turn it upside down. Who do you see now?

An old man.

Playing with Blocks

Which white block is bigger?

If you guessed the top one, guess again. Both blocks are the same size.

Real or Imaginary?

Look carefully at this drawing. While it looks real enough, this object could not actually physically exists. It is an example of what is called an "impossible figure."

Rubbery Columns?

Are these columns bending or straight?

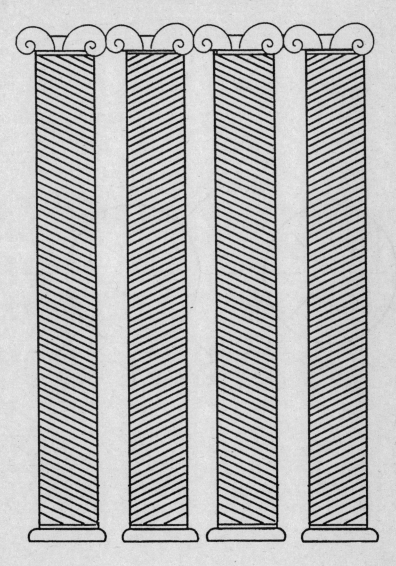

They're perfectly straight, but the diagonal lines make them appear to bend.

Going in Circles

Which circle is larger?

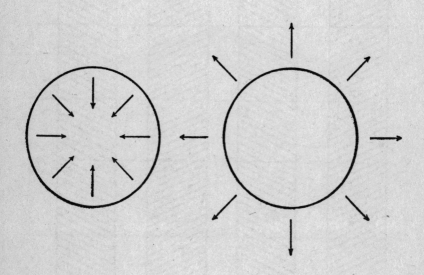

They are exactly the same size. The arrows outside the circle on the right make it appear larger.

To Bend or Not to Bend?

What's unusual about these bending lines?

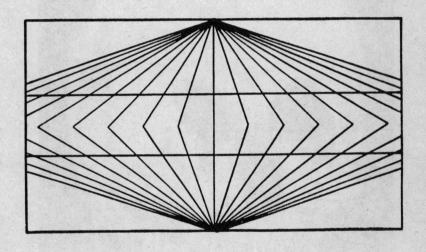

What's unusual is that they're not bending at all: they're perfectly straight and parallel. The lines around them make them look like they're bending.

Mirror, Mirror!

Is this picture merely a lady seated before her mirror . . . or something else?

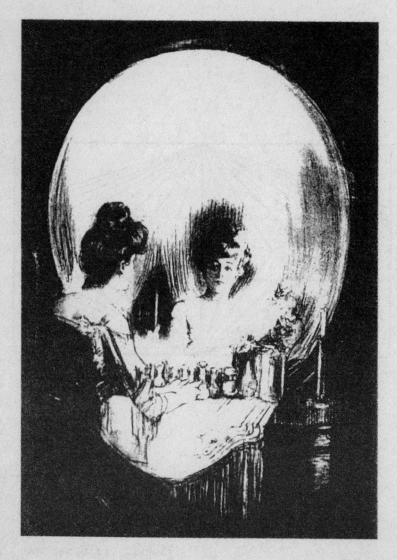

Many people see in this well-known 19th-century print a large white skull.